GAYLORD S

The Mountain Lion

NATURE WALK

NATURE WALK

The Mountain Lion

James V. Bradley

CHELSEA CLUBHOUSE

An Imprint of Chelsea House Publishers

THE MOUNTAIN LION
© 2006 by Infobase Publishing

Chelsea Clubhouse
An imprint of Infobase Publishing
132 West 31st Street
New York NY 10001

Library of Congress Cataloging-in-Publication Data

Bradley, James V. (James Vincent), 1931–
  The mountain lion / James V. Bradley.
      p. cm. — (Nature walk)
  Includes bibliographical references and index.
  ISBN 0-7910-9119-8 (hardcover)
  1. Puma—Juvenile literature. I. Title. II. Series: Bradley, James V.
(James Vincent), 1931– Nature walk.
  QL737.C23B714 2006
  599.75'24—dc22   2006011761

Chelsea House books are available at special discounts when purchased in bulk quantities for businesses, associations, institutions, or sales promotions. Please call our Special Sales Department in New York at (212) 967-8800 or (800) 322-8755.

You can find Chelsea House on the World Wide Web at
http://www.chelseahouse.com

TEXT AND COVER DESIGN by Takeshi Takahashi
ILLUSTRATIONS by William Bradley
SERIES EDITOR Tara Koellhoffer

Printed in the United States of America

BANG PKG 10 9 8 7 6 5 4 3 2 1

This book is printed on acid-free paper.

All links and Web addresses were checked and verified to be correct at the time of publication. Because of the dynamic nature of the Web, some addresses and links may have changed since publication and may no longer be valid.

TABLE OF CONTENTS

Chapter 1

Introduction to the Mountain Lion

The Mountain Lion's Range

BEFORE WHITE SETTLERS MOVED into the Western Hemisphere, the mountain lion's territory covered much of North and South America. Mountain lions (also called cougars) adapted to many habitats ranging from high mountainous terrain to prairies and swamps. Today, because of hunting and the destruction of the mountain lion's habitats, the mountain lion's territory is largely confined to the Western states and Canada, with a small population living in the Florida Everglades. The numbers

The Mountain Lion

Mountain lions are known by many other names, such as *cougars* and *pumas*.

of mountain lions in Mexico, Central America, and South America are not known. Recent sightings indicate that mountain lions are slowly returning to the Midwest. In the year 2004 alone, mountain lions were spotted in Iowa and Oklahoma. Other states with confirmed mountain lion sightings are Missouri, Illinois, Kansas, and Nebraska. There have been unconfirmed sightings in many other states.

Anatomy of the Mountain Lion

The mountain lion's head is small compared to the heads of other larger cats. In the dark, the pupil of the mountain lion's eye is almost round. In bright sunlight, the pupil narrows into a vertical slit that lets less light enter than a round pupil would. The mountain lion's vision at dusk or at night is aided by a layer of cells that reflect any rays of light that go into the eye. This greatly helps the mountain lion detect motion so it can see its prey. The mountain lion's eyes are close together. This gives the mountain lion better **depth perception**. The ears are small and rounded and can turn backwards.

The mountain lion has complete control over the claws in its feet. The claws are like small swords, usually hidden in a sheath in the fur, but they are extended when the mountain lion runs, walks on slippery surfaces, or attacks prey. The claws are curved and extremely sharp. They are excellent tools

CLASSIFYING THE MOUNTAIN LION

While the first branch of the evolution tree gave rise to saber-toothed cats, the second branch gave rise to the cat family Felidae. Two subfamilies represent most of the cat species. Some are listed below.

Felidae
<u>Subfamily Felinae (small cats)</u>
  domestic cat
  wild cat (African, European, Asian, others)
  lynx (Canadian, Eurasian, Iberian, others)
  ocelot
  mountain lion (the largest of the small cats)

<u>Subfamily Pantherine (big cats)</u>
  lion
  jaguar
  leopard
  tiger

for holding prey and tearing flesh, and they allow mountain lions to climb trees with ease.

Mountain lions eat with their heads turned to one side (just as your own house cat does), slicing meat from the bone with molars called **carnassials**. When the jaw closes, the top three carnassials slide over the bottom two, acting like a scissors. The jaws, though powerful, lack the ability to crush large bones. The tongue is very rough. It is an effective tool for licking the meat off bones and for grooming the mountain lion's own fur.

The mountain lion's back legs are longer than its front legs, so the front of the animal is lower than its rear. The powerful back legs are used to knock large prey, like deer, off their feet.

Weight varies with where they live, but male mountain lions average about 130–160 pounds (59–73 kg), and females weigh about 80–120 pounds (36–54 kg). The length of the male, from the nose to the tip of the tail, is about 11 feet (3.4 m). Females are about 8 feet (2.4 m) long.

The mountain lion's long, thick tail is used to help it stay balanced when it runs. The tail has no tuft on the end, like that of a lion. The tip of the tail is dark brown or black. Some experts believe that mountain lion kittens follow their mother by using her tail's black tip as a guide.

The mountain lion's heart and lungs are small, compared to its body weight. It depends on stealth

The pupils of a mountain lion's eyes are almost perfectly round when there is not much light, but in bright sunlight, the pupils narrow into a vertical slit.

and ambush rather than a long pursuit to capture its prey.

Unlike lions, mountain lions do not roar, but they do purr. Mountain lion mothers make various sounds to their kittens. These sounds have been described as chirps and barks. At times, mountain lions will let out a high-pitched scream.

History of the Mountain Lion

With the end of the age of dinosaurs 65 million years ago, the age of mammals began. The empty niches (jobs in a habitat) that were previously occupied by

The mountain lion's tail is thick and strong and helps the mountain lion keep its balance as it moves over rough terrain.

THE MOUNTAIN LION AND THE CRICKET

The lives of American Indian tribes were mixed with the lives of wild animals, which became a part of their religion and art. Many of the stories they told to children involved animals. The following story has probably changed a bit with every telling, but the lesson is clear:

One day, a mountain lion was walking on a log in the forest when a tiny voice came out of the log. It said, "Get off of my log. You are standing on my roof and you will crush my home. Get off of my log, right now!"

The mountain lion was startled by the voice, which came from a little cricket. He lowered his head until his nose was very close to the cricket.

"Who are you to tell *me* what to do?" The mountain lion said. "In this forest, I am chief of the animals."

The cricket replied, "Chief or no chief, I have a cousin who is mightier than you and he will avenge me if you break down my roof."

The mountain lion treated the threat with disgust, saying, "Let your cousin meet me in this place tomorrow, and we shall see who is mightier."

The next day, the mountain lion returned.

"Cricket, where is this mighty cousin of yours? Bring him on! If your cousin does not prove himself to me, I will crush your house with my mighty paw!"

No sooner had the mountain lion spoken than the cricket's cousin, a tiny mosquito, flew up from the log and buzzed inside the mountain lion's ear. Once inside, the mosquito began to bite. The mountain lion batted at his ear with his paw, ran in circles, and dragged his ear on the ground. The cricket asked, "Are you ready to leave my log alone now?"

The mountain lion said yes and the mosquito finally left his ear. Both the cricket and the mosquito watched the mountain lion leave, never to return.

reptiles were now filled by many kinds of mammals. About 35 million years ago, a split occurred in the evolution of cats. One branch gave rise to saber-toothed tigers, and the other gave rise to true felines from the family Felidae, including lions, tigers, bobcats, house cats, and mountain lions, among others.

Saber-toothed "tigers" were not tigers at all, and they were not the ancestors of today's tigers. They went extinct and left no descendants. (*Saber* is another word for "sword.") Their trademark "saber teeth" evolved in true felines and even other kinds of carnivores. For example, in one group were cat-like, saber-toothed **marsupial** carnivores that carried their young in pouches, like kangaroos. All saber-toothed mammals had canine teeth shaped like sabers—long, curved, and flattened on the sides—and all of them are now extinct.

For 35 million years, saber-toothed cats flourished. Many different kinds of these cats evolved as their populations expanded to inhabit much of the Earth. They lived on Earth with **hominids** (human ancestors) for some 7 million years. Some cats undoubtedly came into contact with early hominids and even *Homo sapiens*, our own species, during the last Ice Age, which ended about 10,000 years ago.

The best-known saber-toothed cats were the Smilodons, which lived during the last Ice Age. More than 5,000 fossil bones from Smilodons have been pulled from the La Brea tar pits in Los Angeles, California. The bones of their Ice Age prey— mastodons, hairy mammoths, and giant rhinos and horses—have also been found. Smilodon, the last of the saber-toothed cats, became extinct about 10,000 years ago.

Saber-toothed cats had outstanding success in adapting to changes in climate that occurred on Earth during their 35-million-year-long stay. Like millions of other animal and plant species, they eventually went extinct, but they were not failures. Humans have a long way to go before they will match the success of the saber-toothed cats.

Mountain lions live in all kinds of environments, from wooded areas like this to the forbidding landscape of deserts and mountains.

The first cats to resemble modern cats appeared on Earth 25 million years ago. Cats of many different species have evolved since that time, but they remained small until the first big cats appeared as recently as 2 million years ago. These became the Pantherines—today's lions and tigers.

Although mountain lions are large and have a body pattern like that of the big cats, they belong to the family of small cats, not big cats. Their heads are small compared to their body size, unlike big cats. The structure of the mountain lion's throat also differs from that of the big cats. Lions and tigers can roar, but mountain lions, like all small cats, cannot.

In North America, mountain lions had adapted to live in a wide range of environments, occupying many different habitats: deserts, mountains, prairies, tropical swamps, and hardwood and **coniferous** forests. American Indians had great respect for them and made them part of their culture.

Chapter 2

Mountain Lion Lifestyle

Hunting and Killing Prey

THE MAIN FOOD OF THE mountain lion is large prey, like deer, elk, and moose. However, a mountain lion will also eat smaller prey, such as beavers, woodchucks, rabbits, porcupines, squirrels, coyotes, ducks, geese—almost any animal that is large enough to be worth the energy needed to catch it.

Mountain lions know their territory well, and they know which prey animals are easiest to catch. They make most

18

of their kills in the evening, in the mid-morning, and at night, when deer and elk are on the move.

The most important factor in the mountain lion's attack is cover. A mountain lion depends on stealth to get close to its prey before rushing to attack. As it approaches its prey, the mountain lion will creep forward, keeping its chest close to the ground. This is aided by the extremely flexible movement of the scapula bones (shoulder blades), which are held in place mainly by muscle tissue. Using any available cover—a ditch, a depression, brush, logs, grass—the mountain lion inches forward, never taking its eyes

The mountain lion is an excellent hunter that relies on a swift, silent approach to catch its prey.

off its prey. The closer it can get to its prey, the better its chances for success. If the prey is large, like a bull elk, the mountain lion must get very close to be successful and avoid injury to itself. If the prey is smaller, like a fawn or young elk, the mountain lion may charge from a greater distance. A mountain lion can run over 35 miles (56 km) an hour in short sprints but it cannot run for long distances. Even after a short run, it will pant for some time to recover.

The mountain lion might weigh about 120 pounds (54 kg), while a mule deer, the mountain lion's favorite prey, weighs from 150 to 300 pounds (68 to 136 kg), and elk are even larger. An elk or deer is both heavier and taller, but its body is supported by four long, slender legs. With a successful rush, the mountain lion will knock the prey down. Once down, the prey is doomed.

THE SNEAKY HUNTER

You will probably never witness a mountain lion attacking a deer or elk, but you can see the hunting technique of the mountain lion's close relative, the house cat. When your cat catches a bird or mouse, it uses the same hunting techniques as the mountain lion. The most important of these is stealth—sneaking up on its prey without being seen or heard.

Mountain lions can run very fast, but only for short periods of time before they get tired.

To get ready for a charge, the mountain lion crouches low, bringing its powerful back legs under its body, and then lunges forward. The initial leap can be 20 feet (6 m) or more. After four or five leaps, the mountain lion hits the prey solidly, high on the shoulder. At the moment of impact, the mountain lion's back legs are on the ground, and a forward push adds more force to the blow. With one of the mountain lion's front legs around the base of the neck, the claws dig into the prey's shoulder to keep it from shaking the mountain lion off. The mountain lion's other paw grabs hold of the prey's face or

When attacking prey, a mountain lion will leap up to knock the other animal down.

throat, letting the mountain lion bite into the neck below the head. Usually, the prey crumples and hits the ground with a crash. People who have witnessed a kill report that they heard a loud thud at the moment of impact.

Once down, the prey never has an opportunity to get up again. If the prey is not killed by a neck bite in the initial contact, the mountain lion kills it with another crushing bite to the neck or the throat.

A Dangerous Life

The average mountain lion makes a kill about every 10 days, and a female with kittens kills about every

7 days. Killing prey that can easily be three to five times the mountain lion's weight is a hazardous way to survive. A successful attack depends on many things—the direction of the wind, what kind of cover is available, how alert the prey is—and it is safe to say that the rate of failure is fairly high.

Any mountain lion can misjudge an attack. A young or old mountain lion (old age is around 8 to 10 years old) may be a little bit sloppy in its attack and end up dead or injured. Serious injury that results in an inability to hunt or eat is common for mountain lions. Getting kicked in the jaw, abdomen, or ribs, or being impaled on antlers, can be fatal. If an elk does not go down right away after being hit, it may try to knock the mountain lion off its back by brushing against trees, or may roll over onto the mountain lion. Because it outweighs the mountain lion, it can severely injure the cat.

Eating Habits

Mountain lions are solitary animals, and they usually drag their prey to a secluded place to eat it. Using its claws and teeth, the mountain lion opens up the prey's abdomen and eats the liver, heart, intestines, and other organs. Mountain lions can eat over 15 pounds (6.8 kg) of meat at one feeding. If it has kittens, they join in the feast.

After it eats, the mountain lion covers its kill with leaves and branches and returns to eat more when it

Because they are solitary animals, mountain lions usually bring their food to a secluded location to eat it.

gets hungry. A mountain lion may remain in the same area for a while to guard its food against coyotes, raccoons, and other creatures. After about four or five feedings, only a few bones, hoofs, some skin, and antlers are left. If the meat turns bad, the mountain lion will usually leave it behind and go after another kill.

Chapter 3

Studying
Mountain Lions

The Big Creek Study

IN 1964, FOUR BIOLOGISTS—John Seidensticker, Maurice Hornocker, Wilbur Wiles, and J. P. Messick—started a study of mountain lion populations in the Salmon River Mountains of central Idaho. It was called the Big Creek study. This region of Idaho is made up of nearly 2,000 square miles (5,180 square km) of pristine, rugged mountainous terrain that is home to mule deer (which are larger than white-tailed deer), elk, and mountain goats. Elevation in the areas ranges from 3,000 feet (914 m) along the Salmon River to mountain peaks of over 10,000 feet (3,048 m). The study revealed a great deal about the lifestyle of the mountain lion as well as the methods that wildlife biologists can use to study this elusive animal.

The biologists said, "Our goal was to follow the day-to-day movements of a number of lions simultaneously through summer and winter as they roamed about a vast mountain wilderness." The team of biologists did this by capturing and collaring mountain lions and then mapping their movements with radio tracking. Although radio tracking

The mountain lions of the Big Creek study lived in a mountainous region with steep cliffs.

let the scientists know the general location of the mountain lions, to actually sight the animals they had to follow mountain lion tracks in a wilderness known for its steep canyon walls and rocky slopes along the Salmon River, as well as steep hills with many deep gullies. The biologists also had to cope with hot summer temperatures and rain and, in the winter, "snow that covers most of the big game ranges in depths from a few centimeters to a meter." There have been many sightings of mountain lions throughout the United States. Finding out if these sightings are real often depends on being able to tell the footprints of large dogs from those of mountain lions.

Setting up Camp

Biologists Maurice Hornocker and Wilbur Wiles traveled by foot for over 9,500 miles (15,289 km) between January 1970 and May 1972 as they followed the daily movement of mountain lions. They also set up seven camps from which to observe the mountain lions of the area. Following are some of their observations, discoveries, and adventures.

The biologists wrote: "Lions did not appear to avoid our sign or our camps except when we were in residence with the hounds. We often found where a lion had utilized trails we had broken in the snow only a few hours earlier. We regularly monitored lion

TRACKING MOUNTAIN LIONS

Dog: left front foot
- The two front toe pads of a dog are aligned about side by side.
- Dogs prints often leave nail prints.
- The front heel print of a dog has one bump.
- The back of the heel print of a dog has two bumps.

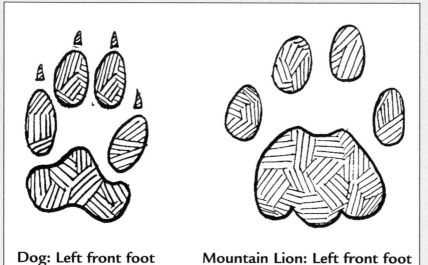

Dog: Left front foot   Mountain Lion: Left front foot

Mountain lion: left front foot (can be 3 to 4 inches [7.6 to 10.2 cm] from toe to heel)
- The two front toe pads of the mountain lion are not aligned.
- The front of the heel pad is slightly curved in, resulting in two small bumps.
- The rear of the heel pad shows three bumps.
- The mountain lion rarely leaves nail prints when walking.

movements from camps where, at times, lions moved to within a few hundred meters. We occasionally found old tracks made through our camps in our absence. In one instance, a female with large kittens killed a cow elk only 30 m [33 yards] from a frequently used camp less than 12 hours after we left."

According to the study, "Even though the mountain lion, *Felis concolor*, is secretive and retiring by nature, men encouraged and motivated by a pioneering antipredator attitude found it was easy prey to capture with traps, and especially with hunting dogs." The biologists used three hounds to chase mountain lions into trees. Then they injected the mountain lions with a drug-filled dart fired from a specially designed gun. They explained, "If drugged lions remained in the tree, we lowered them to the ground by rope. If lions jumped from the tree upon being injected, we approached them on the ground. All lions captured for the first time were marked with numbered, colored, aluminum cattle tags and all were tattooed with an identifying number in both ears."

The mountain lions were then fitted with collars that had radio transmitters attached to them. Radio tracking by light aircraft and hand-held receivers could plot the positions of the lions at various times throughout the summer and winter months. The scientists explained, "With each location, we recorded **elevation**, time, and, when possible, habitat type,

One way the biologists of the Big Creek study caught mountain lions to collar them was by chasing them into trees.

activity, location of big game kills, if present, and association with other radiotagged lions."

During the eight winters they were tracked in the Big Creek study area, 54 mountain lions, including 16 adult males, 14 adult females, and 24 younger lions, were captured and marked. Mountain lions had to be recaptured once a year to replace the batteries in their transmitters. Some tagged mountain lions were recaptured several times. Others were never seen again after the first capture.

The biologists said, "Even with the advantage of our radiotracking methodology, we could rarely see lions. In most instances, it was impossible to tell if the lion was or was not aware of our approach. In some situations, it appeared that the lion froze if it was aware of the investigators' presence. If approached, even at a considerable distance (180 m [197 yards]), the cat sneaked away rapidly. . . . When we surprised a lion by silent approach, the lion usually fled. However when Seidensticker moved in close to [mountain lion] No. 93 in an attempt to determine the exact position of her kill and to determine the size and number of her kittens, she advanced slowly towards him until he threw a stick which broke over her shoulder. She ran back into cover, but remained in the vicinity for 5 more days."

Tracking the Mountain Lions

The timing of tracking for any particular lion depended on the weather, the number of lions to be located, the need to find individual lions, and how much money the scientists could spend on the study. At a certain date, a mountain lion might be at Point A and days or weeks later it might be at Point B. The actual route the mountain lion took to get from one place to another could not be plotted.

The biologists explained, "Lions seldom traveled frozen waterways and trails as did coyotes wintering

Mountain lions prefer to be hidden by trees or other cover and rarely move into wide open spaces.

in the same area. Usually lions zigzagged back and forth through thickets, moved around large openings, under rock overhangs, up and down little draws (ditches), and back and forth across creeks. The impression we gained in snow tracking lions was that through this procedure they were better able to detect prey animals and launch a successful attack."

Seeing a mountain lion move through a boulder field or over a mountain slope covered with logs and fallen trees with ease and grace is a real treat. Mountain lions always take advantage of whatever cover is available and only rarely expose themselves in open areas. They seek shelter or are less active in heavy rain, but they don't seem to be bothered by light rain or snow.

SCIENTIFIC STUDIES OF MOUNTAIN LIONS

Mountain lions in the wild are not easy to study. So, scientists who study animal behavior have to rely on direct observation (seeing actual kills and encounters between mountain lions, for example) and indirect observation (radio tracking, tracking in snow, studying the locations and conditions of food supplies). A knowledge of the habits of close relatives, like the house cat and bobcat, is useful. Much of what was learned in the Big Creek study came from interpreting the tracks of mountain lions in snow.

Another Mountain Lion Study

In a 10-year study started in the 1980s, Ken Logan and Linda Sweanor studied mountain lions in the mountains of New Mexico. Their findings were quite different from those of the Big Creek study. They found that mountain lions were much more aggressive than those in the Big Creek study, with frequent fights over territory that resulted in serious injury. Fights between males were especially vicious, with some resulting in death. The increased aggression was probably because of the competition for prey due to the loss of habitat. Hunger can cause any animal to act aggressively.

Chapter 4

Mountain Lion Homes

Home Areas

THE BIG CREEK STUDY showed that specific home areas are a large part of the mountain lion's social behavior. A mountain lion will claim a home area that meets its needs for food, shelter, and **reproduction**. Once it has a home area, it will generally stay there. Home areas are fairly stable: Some mountain lions returned to their summer area for three years in a row, but they may move when neighboring mountain lions die or when prey is hard to find. The size of the home area varies. It may

range from 50 square miles to 500 square miles
(129.5 to 1,295 square km).

A mountain lion gets to know its home area very
well. It knows where there are good places to hunt. It
knows where there are good lookouts for watching
deer and elk. And it knows where there are hidden
places for sleeping or raising young, and areas that
have dense, rugged cover, such as a boulder field,
where humans or dogs would have difficulty following it.

As winter comes, the deer and elk move to lower
altitudes and the mountain lion leaves to follow its

Mountain lions get to know their home areas very well, and
know the best spots to go to watch for prey.

In the winter, mountain lions follow their prey to lower altitudes—ground that is not high in the mountains.

prey. The mountain lion's winter area may be much smaller than the place it spends its summers.

Radio tracking has shown that the home areas of males do not overlap with those of other males, but male areas do overlap females' areas. In contrast, female areas frequently overlap with those of other females. Even with overlap of home areas, mountain lions avoid contact with each other.

With the home area system, each mountain lion has enough game to keep it alive. It also ensures that females have males available when they are ready to mate. Establishing a home area helps give the female

DEALING WITH INTRUDERS

You might expect that if a male lion found another mountain lion trespassing in its home area, an angry exchange would take place and the intruder would either run off or a fight would result in injury or death. This is true for grizzly bears, bobcats, and wolves, but not mountain lions. Mountain lions are solitary animals and take care to avoid entering the territory of other mountain lions.

mountain lion a much better chance of success in raising her young. It is a social system that is part of the mountain lion's **instinct**, and every mountain lion knows to beware of entering the home areas of others. The mountain lion's territorial system depends more on getting along than aggression.

Claiming a Home Area

When a male mountain lion finds a suitable home area, he lets other mountain lions know about his presence. "Urine, scrapes, feces, and scent from anal glands could all serve to advertise a lion's presence and serve to bring lions together or to maintain distance," the Big Creek biologists found. The male makes its presence known mainly through scent, rather than sight or sound. The most common method for letting other lions know that this area is occupied

Mountain lions make their presence known by rubbing or scraping their scent in key places around their home areas.

by a resident lion is the **scrape**. Scrapes are visual signs of occupation that are made on the forest floor. The male will claw at the ground, pulling soil toward itself to create a rectangular trench about 1 to 2 inches (2.5 to 5 cm) deep and roughly 6 inches (15 cm) wide and 14 inches (35.6 cm) long. The male will then urinate or defecate on the pile of soil in front of the trench. The entire structure is called a scrape. Scrapes can be found throughout a mountain lion's home area but, as you might expect, they are most common on the outer boundaries. They are often found several feet from a tree, on rocky ledges and in places where mountain lions are likely to cross the boundary of the home area. Females seldom make scrapes. In fact, they take care not to advertise their presence, especially if they have kittens.

When a mountain lion sniffs at the scrape of another mountain lion, it makes an unusual facial expression. Its lips curl up, exposing its teeth, with its mouth slightly opened. Its face looks as if the mountain lion is going to sneeze. This expression helps force the odor of the scrape back toward the roof of the mouth, where special cells analyze the odors. For example, the mountain lion can detect special odors that tell a male when a female is ready to mate.

The "rules" governing home areas have evolved through thousands of generations to establish a

When a mountain lion smells the scent of another mountain lion, it makes a strange face. This look helps the mountain lion better capture the scent of the other animal.

system that is important to the mountain lion's survival. The system centers around the mountain lion's strong instinct to avoid contact with other mountain lions. It is part of their nature. This **mutual avoidance response** maintains distance between mountain lions. When two mountain lions do meet, the intruder will usually retreat without any physical contact being made. More serious encounters resulting in violence do occur, but they are rare. Throughout the entire eight-year study of the Big Creek mountain lion population, no evidence of scars or injuries inflicted from fighting were seen on the captured mountain lions.

Chapter 5

Mountain Lion Family Life

Finding a Mate

A FEMALE MOUNTAIN LION will not be ready to mate or have young until she has established her own home area. This usually happens when she is three years old or older. Mating can occur any time of the year. Kittens may even be born in the middle of winter.

When a female mountain lion is prepared to have her young, she actively seeks a male with which to mate. She attracts a male by making sharp, high-pitched barks; by rubbing against trees and rocks to leave her scent;

When a female mountain lion is ready to mate, she seeks out a male.

and by spraying urine in noticeable places. At times, she may let out a high-pitched scream to attract a male. The scream has been described as shattering and frightening, and has become part of early American folklore.

The female's urine contains chemicals that let the male know she is ready to mate. Sometimes the male and female meet before the female is ready. In this case, the female will swat the male with her front paw if he comes toward her. The male will then wait, but will not leave, until the female is ready.

Building a Family

The human family structure of male, female, and offspring does not apply to mountain lions. After mating, the male leaves and takes no part in raising the kittens. His job in this reproductive scheme is to father as many offspring with as many females as possible. The mountain lion family is made up of the female and her kittens. The female mates with only one male in any one season, and then she goes back to her normal solo life in her home area. She will protect, raise, and feed her kittens for a year and a half to two years.

A female mountain lion is pregnant for 86 to 96 days. When the time comes to give birth, the mountain lion settles in a place that offers shelter from the weather and predators. For example, she might

After mating, the male mountain lion does not play a role in raising the offspring.

choose the base of a cliff under a rocky ledge—a place that offers some protection from wind and rain but is exposed to the early sun for warmth. The average number of kittens is two or three, but can be as high as six or as low as one.

Mountain lion kittens start to nurse immediately after birth. They open their eyes in 10 to 14 days, and their eyes are light blue. They have spotted coats and short tails, and they huddle together to stay warm. Like all members of the genus *Felis*, both kittens and the female mountain lion will purr as a sign of contentment. The kittens remain behind in their den while their mother hunts.

Kittens Play and Learn

Well-fed mountain lion kittens are bundles of curiosity. They are always exploring their surroundings, catching butterflies or beetles, jumping on a flower or a sibling, or biting their mother's tail. It is easy to see how their play helps them learn basic skills: One kitten will lie in wait for its sibling to pass and then attack. Other times, a kitten will ambush its mother's twitching tail. Two kittens will wrestle, using their legs and paws. An overexcited bite on the ear may bring a sharp yelp from a sibling.

Mountain lion kittens have blue eyes and spots on their fur.

Within a short time, the kittens begin to venture farther away from the den, but they always stay within sight of their mother. At times, the mother will lead them on short trips. Using barks and chirps, she teaches them to come when they are called and to hide and take cover.

The kittens nurse for five to six weeks and then they are gradually introduced to solid food. The mother will bring in a rabbit, squirrel, or other small animal for the kittens to eat. They rip and tear, competing with each other to get the best pieces.

Young mountain lions learn the skills they need for survival by exploring their environment and playing with their siblings.

With all their activity and noise, dens often attract predators. To avoid predators, the mother mountain lion often changes sites, carrying each kitten by its head from one site to another.

About eight weeks after they are born, the kittens begin to follow their mother on hunting trips. They learn to respond to her call to follow, and her call to run and hide. They learn to hunt by observing their mother, and they also learn the dangers of meeting with porcupines, rattlesnakes, and eagles.

A Dangerous Childhood

Death rates for young kittens are not known, but they are probably high. Young mountain lions face many dangers. One of these dangers actually comes from the male mountain lion. Males will instinctively kill mountain lion kittens, and have been known to eat them. The male—even the mate of the female—kills kittens in order to encourage the female to have more young. Coyotes, bears, badgers, bald eagles, and a host of other predators are also ever-present threats that help account for the high death rate of kittens.

Most western states have laws to regulate the hunting of mountain lions. Most states have no laws against killing female mountain lions, and in those that do, it's hard to make sure people follow the law. Mountain lions are hunted with dogs that are set loose to follow fresh mountain lion tracks. Usually, the mountain lion will get tired quickly and hide in a tree. Mountain lions have used this tactic for thousands of years to avoid packs of wolves. The hunter then simply shoots the mountain lion out of the tree. If it is a female with kittens, any young mountain lions that have not yet learned how to kill large prey will starve.

Growing Up as a Mountain Lion

In about a year, the kittens have grown in size and look more like adults, having lost most of their spots. They will stay with their mother for a year and a half to two years. A female with three large kittens has to kill one deer about every three days. This is a time when the female is under a lot of pressure to feed her young. As the kittens grow, they can travel greater distances to hunt, and the kittens can capture small animals on their own and even try to hunt larger animals. Some scientists believe that when the kittens reach a certain size, the female will take only a single kitten out to hunt at a time.

The kittens learn by watching as their mother brings down deer and elk as well as smaller animals and birds. Mountain lions learn that when waterfowl are **molting** they are unable to fly, making them easier to catch. Sometimes they even get lucky and snag a bird out of the air. Mountain lions can leap 12 feet (3.7 m) in the air. When the juveniles (young lions)

About a year after they are born, mountain lion kittens lose their spots and look almost like adults.

leave their mother, they have no one but themselves to depend on. A juvenile who is not skilled in hunting gets weak from hunger, and weakness increases the chance for failure.

When confronted by another mountain lion, a black bear, or any other predator, the female will fight to defend her kittens. In such situations, the mountain lion's goal is not to kill the predator but to make it as miserable as possible. Mountain lions know that any injury that harms their ability to hunt usually leads to death. In such confrontations, the female mountain lion is fast and nimble, and she uses these skills to distract the predator and keep it away from the kittens. In most cases, the predator will not risk injury for such a small meal and will back away.

Transient Mountain Lions

When her kittens reach the age of one and a half to two years, the mother will break her bonds with them, for they are now almost fully grown. She usually does this by leaving them at the site of a kill. When she does not return, the kittens wander off on their own. A pair of siblings, especially males, will sometimes team up for several weeks, but they, too, will separate to become **transients** looking to claim a home area.

The resident female remains in her home area and, within several weeks, will be ready to mate again. It is possible for a female to have five pregnancies within her lifetime.

Sometimes, a female transient will remain in the mother's home area for a short time. If a nearby area becomes vacant, she may claim it. Females do not range as far as males and will not go into estrus until they are secure in their own home areas.

Males do not usually have home areas that overlap with the home areas of other males. If the male is lucky enough to find a vacant area, he will take it. If he finds an area occupied by an old or injured lion, he may challenge the resident to a fight. The winner gets the territory.

Chapter 6

Mountain Lions and People

Losing Their Habitats

STATISTICS SHOW THAT THERE were 67 reported non-fatal mountain lion attacks on people and 11 fatal attacks from 1990 to 2004 in the United States and Canada. This count is not exact because some reports are not recorded and others are exaggerated, but it is accurate enough to show that there has been an increase in the number of people who come into contact with mountain lions. This is not surprising when you consider that the mountain lion's habitat is being destroyed, especially in California and throughout much of the West. For example, the foothills of the Rocky Mountains in Colorado, formerly mountain lion country, are quickly being covered up by housing developments.

For several years, 20 mountain lions in and around the Cuyamaca Rancho State Park, 35 miles (56 km) east of San Diego, have been tracked using **global positioning collars**. What surprised investigators was how well mountain lions adapted to human activity while still remaining unseen. During the day, mountain lions sometimes slept within a few hundred

Mountain lions are fierce, skilled hunters. The victim rarely sees the attack coming before it is too late.

feet of major hiking trails. The mountain lion's movements were mostly **nocturnal** and involved crossing interstate highways and skirting clusters of homes. Some ranch workers never realized that losses of goats and cattle were caused by roaming mountain lions.

Mountain Lion Attacks

With the loss of habitat, some mountain lions, especially transients that are looking for home areas of their own, will come into contact with humans. Mountain lions that attack people are often juveniles that are not skilled in hunting, or older, injured lions. To a mountain lion, you are just another link in the **food chain**. Mountain lions use the same hunting technique on humans that they use to take down deer or elk. They are very quick to detect the slightest weakness that might give them an advantage. They prefer easy prey, such as a hiker walking alone.

What to Do if You Meet a Mountain Lion

A can of pepper spray is good to have while hiking or camping, and a strong stick is, too. These will both help if you encounter a mountain lion.

If the mountain lion is some distance away and seems to be tracking you, walk slowly, talk loudly and firmly, and stay close to adults. More than 50 percent of attacks involve children under 16 years old. Along the way, look for heavy sticks, rocks, or anything you might be able to use as a weapon, but don't bend down to pick these up if the lion is close. Being higher than the mountain lion gives you an advantage. If possible, move into open land, away from trees.

You can tell that a mountain lion is preparing to attack when it is nearby with its belly close to the ground, its back legs under its body, and the furry sides of its ears facing you. Mountain lions are not used to humans. If a person fights hard, a mountain lion will usually give up and run away.

Mountain lion attacks are not common compared to some other animal attacks. For example, on aver-

A mountain lion prepares to attack by putting its belly close to the ground, then it springs toward its prey.

age, there are 12 fatal dog attacks each year. In the year 2001, more than 368,000 patients were treated in emergency rooms for nonfatal dog bites.

Seeing a mountain lion is very rare; being attacked by one is even more unusual. Many thousands of people camp out in mountain lion country every year and never even see a mountain lion. As with all wild animals, though, you should be careful to respect it and its habitat. Then it will respect you.

altitudes—Measures of how high a place is, usually compared to sea level.

carnassials—Teeth in meat-eating animals that are specially adapted for cutting rather than tearing.

coniferous—Referring to mostly evergreen trees that have needle-shaped or scale-like leaves.

depth perception—The ability to judge how far away objects are.

elevation—The height of a place above the level of the sea; the altitude.

food chain—A hierarchy of living things within the same habitat. At the top are predators, in the middle are the prey of these predators, and at bottom are the plants and insects that both the prey and predators eat.

global positioning collars—Devices equipped with global positioning systems (GPS), which use satellite signals to pinpoint the location of the person or thing carrying the device.

hominids—Members of a family of primates that walk on two legs. Hominids include humans and their extinct ancestors.

instinct—A natural response to a particular situation.

marsupial—An animal that is part of an order of mammals that includes kangaroos, wombats, and opossums.

molting—A state in which birds shed their feathers before growing new ones.

mutual avoidance response—The mountain lion's instinctual habit of avoiding other mountain lions.

nocturnal—Active at night.

reproduction—The process of creating offspring.

scrape—A marking in the soil that is used to indicate that an area has been claimed by a particular mountain lion.

transients—Mountain lions that have not yet claimed a home area.

BIBLIOGRAPHY

Beier, P. "Mountain Lion Attacks on Humans in the United States and Canada." *Wildlife Society* Bulletin 19(1991): 403–412.

Ewer, R. F. *The Carnivores*. Ithaca, NY: Cornell University Press, 1973.

Gonyea, W. J. "The Form and Function of Retractile Claws in the Felidae and Other Representative Carnivorans." *Journal of Mammology* 40 (1975): 481–495.

Hansen, Kevin. *Mountain Lion: The American Lion*. Flagstaff, AZ: North Publishing Company.

Hornocker, M. G. "Winter Territoriality in Mountain Lions." *The Journal of Wildlife Management* 33(3)(1969).

McCafferty, Keith. "The Face of Danger." *Field and Stream*, December 2003–January 2004.

Seidensticker, John C., IV, Maurice G. Hornocker, Wilbur V. Wiles, and John P. Messick. "Mountain Lion Social Organization in the Idaho Primitive Area." *Wildlife Monograph* 35 (1973): 15.

Turner, Alan, and Mauricio Anton. *The Big Cats and Their Fossil Relatives*. New York: Columbia University Press.

Bolgiano, Chris. *Mountain Lion: An Unnatural History of Pumas and People*. Mechanicsburg, PA: Stackpole Books, 2001.

Busch, Robert H. *The Cougar Almanac: A Complete Natural History of the Mountain Lion*. Guilford, CT: The Lyons Press, 2004.

Etling, Kathy. *Cougar Attacks: Encounters of the Worst Kind*. Guilford, CT: The Lyons Press, 2001.

Kobalenko, Jerry. *Forest Cats of North America: Cougars, Bobcats, Lynx*. Ontario, Canada: Firefly Books Ltd., 2005.

Shaw, Harley G. *Soul Among Lions: The Cougar As Peaceful Adversary*. Tucson, AZ: University of Arizona Press, 2000.

Web Sites

Cat Action Treasury
www.felidae.org/

Mountain Lion/Cougar, DesertUSA
www.desertusa.com/may96/du_mlion.html

Mountain Lions
www.mountain-lions.org/

The Mountain Lion Foundation
www.mountainlion.org/

PICTURE CREDITS

ABOUT THE AUTHOR

James V. Bradley taught biology at Lake Forest High School in Lake Forest, Illinois, for 25 years. He also taught science in Colorado and in the United Kingdom. Bradley received the Illinois STAR Award (Science Teaching Achievement Recognition) in 1980 and was named by the National Association of Biology Teachers as outstanding biology teacher in Illinois in 1981. He retired from teaching in 1994, but continues to write and study science topics.